Know your traffic signs

Department of the Environment, Transport and the Regions

London: The Stationery Office

Introduction

Knowing your traffic signs can be a matter of life and death – yours or somebody else's. It takes a wide variety of signs, signals and road markings to convey quickly and accurately the wide range of information that drivers need. Although the Highway Code shows most of the commonly used signs which are prescribed by the Traffic Signs Regulations, it does not give a comprehensive explanation of our signing system. The aim of this booklet, therefore, is to illustrate and explain the vast majority of traffic signs the road user is likely to encounter.

Since the first edition of *Know Your Traffic Signs* was published in 1975, about 760,000 copies have been sold. This fourth edition takes account of the many changes brought about by the 1994 Traffic Signs Regulations.

New signs, or changed designs, included for the first time in this booklet are marked with an asterisk ★.

Contents

The History of Traffic Signs

It was probably the Romans who first used 'traffic signs' in Britain. They marked their roads with stones which were called 'milliaries'. These marked off distances of one thousand paces (about one mile) with some stones being larger and showing distances to settlements etc. The word 'mile' probably originates from the 'milliary'.

The origin of signposts is obscure since there are very few references to them in history books. Most early signposts were erected by private individuals at their own expense and some of these signs can still be seen around the countryside. A law was passed in 1648 requiring each Parish to place guide posts at its crossroads, but it was not until after the General Turnpike Act of 1773, which imposed a duty on Turnpike Trusts to erect and maintain signposts, that these 'guides' or 'fingerposts' became more common.

The 1773 Act also made it necessary to set up mile posts for the charging of tolls, but the mile did not become a standard measurement until 1864.

This was necessary because some of the Turnpike Trusts, whose tolls were levied on a per mile basis, had been interpreting the distance to their own advantage.

During the latter part of the nineteenth century the increasing popularity of the bicycle brought recognition of new hazards to road users and it was considered that new signs were needed. Steep hills and sharp bends were very dangerous to early cyclists and 'danger' and 'caution' signs were erected at the top of steep hills. Signs showing a skull and crossbones were erected at the most dangerous places. Local authorities and cycling organisations installed an estimated 4,000 warning signs, which eventually began to lose their effectiveness because of over-use.

The ending of the 'red flag' requirement in 1896 heralded the era of the motor car and some motoring associations took up the business of placing signs. The Motor Car Act of 1903 made local authorities responsible for placing certain warning and prohibitory signs. The signs were for crossroads, steep hills and dangerous bends. A hollow red triangle indicated a warning sign and a solid red disc signified prohibitions. Speed limit signs had a hollow white ring above the plate giving the speed limit in figures. Other notices were on diamond shaped boards.

'A' and 'B' numbering of roads was introduced in 1921 and these numbers were shown on finger post style signs alongside the destination and distance. Town or village name signs and warning signs for schools, level crossings and double bends were introduced at the same time.

The main task of signposting our roads during the first 30 years of this century still fell on the motoring organisations. By 1931 it was realised that the pace of development of motor cars had outstripped that of the signing system. A committee was set up to consider improvements and by 1933 further new signs began to appear including 'No entry' and 'Keep left' signs, warning signs for narrow roads and bridges, low bridges, roundabouts and hospitals. Other signs followed during the 1930s including 'Halt at major road ahead'. These formed the basis of our road signing until the early 1960s.

The origin of road markings is rather obscure but, in a publication of 1843, the use of a centre line of white stones and lamps was advocated. However, it was not until after the First World War that white lines actually began to appear on British roads, and later during the 1920s their use spread rapidly. In 1926 the first Ministry of Transport circular on the subject was issued, and this laid down general principles on the use of white lines. In the 1930s white lines were used as 'stop' lines at road junctions controlled either by police or by traffic lights, for marking the course to be taken at bends, junctions and corners and also for indicating the proximity of refuges and other obstacles in the carriageway.

Reflecting road studs (sometimes referred to as 'cat's-eyes') first came into use in 1934 and it has been estimated that there are about seven million studs of various types in use at the present time in Britain.

By 1944, white lines were also being used to indicate traffic lanes and to define the boundary of the main carriageway at entrances to side roads and laybys, and in conjunction with 'halt' signs.

Experiments to control overtaking by the use of double white lines were first made in 1957. These generally proved successful and in 1959 regulations came into effect giving legal force to the system.

After the Second World War, discussions took place in the United Nations on the introduction of international traffic signs. Most European countries agreed to use them, but in the United Kingdom we felt some reluctance to change our well-established system. One reason for this was the possibility, at that time, that the European system might be replaced by a different World system.

When the motorway construction programme began, the direction signs prescribed in the 1957 Regulations were not considered adequate for use on high speed dual carriageway roads. A Committee was set up in 1958 under the chairmanship of Sir Colin Anderson to consider new designs for motorway signs. The Committee's recommendation of blue background signs, as used in some European countries, was accepted. The now familiar motorway symbol was modified from a design adopted by the United Nations Inland Transport Committee.

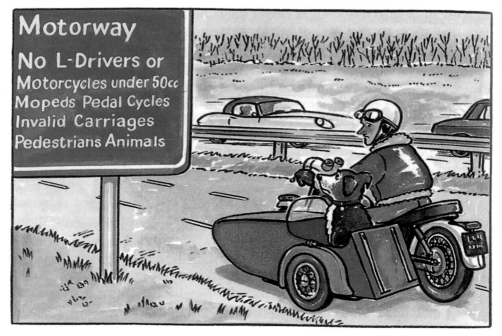

Growing general criticism of the inadequacy of the British traffic signs system for modern traffic conditions led to the appointment, in 1961, of a new Committee under the chairmanship of Sir Walter Worboys to review the complete system. As a result of their studies, this Committee concluded that the United Kingdom should adopt the main principles of the European system. The recommendations of the Committee were accepted and in 1964 we fell into line with European practice on traffic signs. Work began on the conversion of signs in 1965, and this is the basic system that we still have in use today.

The provision of new signs is a continuous process. As the volume and type of traffic on our roads change, ways of giving essential information to drivers and improving traffic flow and road safety have to be reviewed. New signs and road markings are well and truly tested at certain locations to demonstrate their effectiveness before their wide-scale use is recommended. Such experiments have led to the introduction of yellow box markings at congested road junctions, special signals and road markings at pedestrian crossings and signs and markings to indicate mini-roundabouts and bus lanes.

Developments in other areas also make it necessary to revise traffic signs. Following pressure from the freight industry and the police, the basis for controlling the movement of heavy goods vehicles was changed in 1981 from unladen weight to maximum gross weight and at the same time, to continue the move towards the European system of signing, the weights used were changed from the imperial 'ton' to the metric 'tonne' indicated by the letter 'T' on signs. Similarly, signs for weak bridges are now expressed in terms of maximum gross weight rather than axle weight or the actual weight of the vehicle and its load. The re-introduction of trams onto the streets of Manchester and Sheffield has resulted in the development of a new range of signs and signals. Attempts to reduce the number of accidents at railway level crossings and low bridges have led to improved methods of signing and signalling.

Increased tourist traffic created an increased demand for more signs showing the way to specific places of interest and to local facilities. Direction signs with white lettering on a brown background and often incorporating symbols indicating the nature of the attraction are now being used for this purpose.

The latest Regulations published in 1994 continue the same principles but include some new regulatory and warning signs. They also introduced simplifications in the yellow line system of waiting restrictions, which it was considered had become too complex.

These Regulations introduced some significant changes to direction signs which extended the well established system of direction signs on routes being colour coded to reflect the status of the road. These changes follow from a review of direction signs in 1987 and subsequent experiment in Guildford, Surrey.

More use is being made of new technology to provide better information to drivers on hazards, delays and diversions on variable message signs.

It is estimated that there are about 2,500,000 upright signs and signals on the roads in England today and about 850,000 road markings of various types. The future will undoubtedly see more developments in traffic signing to keep pace with the changing traffic demands on our roads.

New signs, or changed designs, included for the first time in this booklet are marked with an asterisk ★.

The Signing System

There are three basic types of traffic signs. Signs which give orders, signs that warn and signs which give information. Each type has a different shape.

Circles
give orders

Triangles
warn

Rectangles
inform

A further guide to the function of a sign is its colour.

Blue circles tell you what you must do

Red rings or circles tell you what you must not do, eg, you must not exceed 30 mph, no vehicles over the height shown may proceed

Blue rectangles are used for information signs **except** on motorways where blue is used for direction signs

Green rectangles are used for direction signs on primary routes

White rectangles with black borders are used to show directions on non-primary routes

There are a few exceptions to the shape and colour rules to give greater prominence to certain signs. For example, the octagonal stop sign.

Warning Signs

(other than those for railway and tramway level crossings, bus and pedal cycle facilities, and road works)

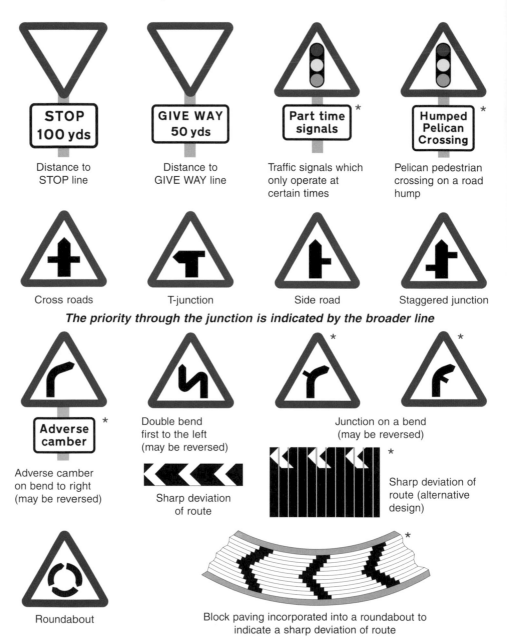

STOP 100 yds — Distance to STOP line

GIVE WAY 50 yds — Distance to GIVE WAY line

Part time signals * — Traffic signals which only operate at certain times

Humped Pelican Crossing * — Pelican pedestrian crossing on a road hump

Cross roads

T-junction

Side road

Staggered junction

The priority through the junction is indicated by the broader line

Adverse camber * — Adverse camber on bend to right (may be reversed)

Double bend first to the left (may be reversed)

Junction on a bend * (may be reversed)

Sharp deviation of route

Sharp deviation of route (alternative design) *

Roundabout

Block paving incorporated into a roundabout to indicate a sharp deviation of route *

REDUCE SPEED NOW

Reduction in speed necessary for change in road layout

Road narrows on both sides

Road narrows on right (left if symbol reversed)

Plates used with "Road narrows" signs

Oncoming vehicles in middle of road

Single file traffic

Single file traffic in each direction

Single track road

Road only wide enough for one line of vehicles

Dual carriageway ends

Two-way traffic

Two-way traffic on route crossing ahead

Worded warning sign

Steep hill upwards

Steep hill downwards

*

Sign used with "Steep hill downwards" or "Try brakes"

Try brakes after crossing a ford or before descending a steep hill

Plates used with "Steep hill" signs

Low gear for 1½ miles

Low gear now

Keep in low gear

Slippery road

Side winds

Uneven road

Road humps for distance shown

Risk of ice (may be varied to snowdrifts)

Soft verges for distance shown

Other danger.
The plate indicates the nature of the danger

and in direction indicated

Tunnel

Opening or swing bridge

Hump bridge

Road hump in direction indicated and at the distance shown

End of bridge parapet, abutment wall, tunnel mouth etc

Risk of falling or fallen rocks

Quayside or riverbank

Nearside edge of carriageway or obstruction near that edge (white markers are used on the offside edge and amber ones on the offside edge of a dual carriageway)

Distance to hazard

Distance and direction to hazard

Distance over which hazard extends

School

Children going
to or from school

Pedestrian
crossing

**Elderly
people**

Elderly pedestrians
likely to cross
("Elderly" may be
varied to "Blind"
or "Disabled")

**No footway
for 400 yds**

Pedestrians in
road for distance
shown

Playground

Children's
playground

**Humped
Zebra
Crossing**

Zebra crossing
on a road hump

Low flying
helicopters or
sudden helicopter
noise

Low flying aircraft
or sudden aircraft
noise

**Disabled
children** *

Disabled children
(may be varied to
"Blind or Deaf")

Gliders *

Gliders likely

Patrol

School crossing
patrol

Lights warning of
children likely to be
crossing the road on
their way to or from
school

! *

**FIRE
STATION**

**STOP
when
lights show**

Warning of signals
("FIRE" may be
varied to
"AMBULANCE")

**Slow lorries
for 2 miles**

Slow moving
vehicles likely for
distance shown

Slow moving
military vehicles likely
to be crossing or in
the road

Accompanied
horses or ponies

Wild horses
or ponies

Migratory toad
crossing

Wild animals

Wild fowl

Sheep

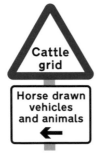

Bypass of
cattle grid

Supervised
cattle crossing

Cattle

Agricultural
vehicles

Supervised cattle
crossing ahead

Area infected
by animal disease

Regulatory Signs

(other than those for railway and tramway level crossings, bus and pedal cycle facilities, and road works)

Most regulatory signs are circular; a **RED RING** or **RED CIRCLE** gives a negative (prohibitory) instruction; a **BLUE CIRCLE** gives a positive (mandatory) instruction.

Two notable exceptions are:

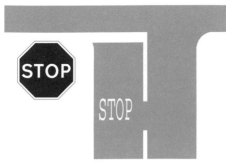

No entry for vehicular traffic

No vehicles except bicycles being pushed by hand:

The **"STOP"** sign and road markings; you **must** stop before crossing the transverse line on the road and ensure the way is clear before entering the major road.

No motor vehicles

– during times shown, except for access

and

*

No motorcycles

Play Street 8 am to sunset except for access

– allowed in "Play Street" during times shown except for access

The **"GIVE WAY"** sign and road markings (the upright sign and triangle on the road are not used at junctions where there is relatively little traffic). You **must** give way at the line to traffic on the major road.

No motor vehicles except motorcycles without sidecars

No horse drawn
vehicles

No ridden or
accompanied horses

No pedestrians

No articulated
vehicles

No vehicles over
maximum width shown

No vehicles or
combinations of
vehicles over
maximum length
shown

No goods vehicles
over maximum
gross weight shown
in tonnes

End of goods
vehicles prohibition

Plates used to indicate exemptions

Except for loading
and unloading
goods vehicles

Except for access
to premises or
land adjacent to
the road, where
there is no other
route

No vehicles over the
maximum gross weight
shown. The bottom plate
is used where empty
vehicles are exempt

Where changes of direction are prohibited a red bar across the sign face is used in
addition to the red circle

No U turn

No right turn

No left turn

No motor vehicles, cycles, animals, pedestrians on mown verge

Specified traffic must not use verge maintained in mown or ornamental condition

No overtaking

Give way to oncoming vehicles *

Priority must be given to vehicles from the other direction

Vehicles must not go beyond the sign where displayed by a police officer or traffic warden

*

Vehicles must not go beyond the sign where displayed by a School Crossing Patrol

One way traffic

Keep left (right if symbol is reversed)

Proceed in direction indicated by the arrow

Turn left ahead (right if symbol is reversed)

Mini-roundabout (give way to traffic from the immediate right)

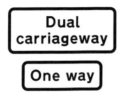

Dual carriageway

One way

Plates supplementing "turn" signs

Vehicles may pass either side to reach the same destination

Vehicles may park partially
on the verge or footway

Vehicles may park partially
on the verge or footway
during the times shown

*

Vehicles may park wholly
on the verge or footway

*

Vehicles may park wholly
on the verge or footway
during the times shown

End of area where
vehicles may park partially
on the verge or footway

*

End of area where vehicles
may park wholly on the
verge or footway

Nature of and distance
to a prohibition, restriction
of requirement

*

Weight restriction ahead

Speed Limit Signs

Remember that in areas of street lighting (other than on motorways) a 30 mph limit applies **unless** another limit is specifically signed.

The maximum speed at which traffic may travel, if it is safe to do so.

The national speed limit for the type of road and class of traffic applies

 *

Advisory speed limit at a bend or other hazard

Traffic must not travel at speeds less than the minimum shown unless it is unsafe or impracticable to do so

The end of a minimum speed requirement

 *

Entrance to a zone where a 20 mph speed limit is in force with traffic calming measures

 *

End of a 20 mph speed limit and return to 30 mph restriction

Low Bridge Signs

Each year there are hundreds of incidents in which bridges are struck by vehicles which are too high to pass under them. Both rail and road users have been killed in these incidents. Look out for the signs in this section and **make sure that you are not a bridge basher.**

All bridges with a clearance of less than 16 feet 6 inches (about 5 metres) are normally signed. Both regulatory roundels and warning triangles can be used depending on the type of bridge.

 *

Bridges particularly at risk from strikes may have a variable message sign which is activated by high vehicles passing through an infra-red beam detector. When the sign is activated, 4 amber lanterns flash, the top pair alternating with the bottom pair.

Regulatory Signs

 *

No vehicles over the height shown may pass the sign. (Height shown in metric and imperial units)

No vehicles over the height shown may pass the sign. (Height shown in imperial units)

 *

Advance warning of a mandatory height restriction ahead; the sign may include an arrow, if the restriction is on a side road

Warning Signs

Signs indicating the maximum safe headroom under a bridge or other overhead obstruction. The sign showing the height in imperial units must be used; an additional sign showing the height in metric may be used.

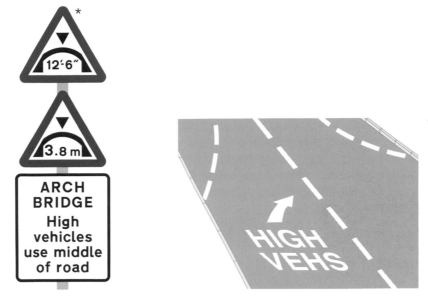

Special signs indicating the maximum safe headroom may be used in advance of arch bridges . . .

together with road markings to guide high vehicles through the highest part of the arch.

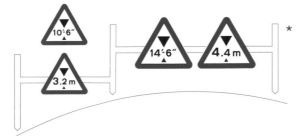

Chord markings used to indicate the points between which different headrooms over different parts of an arch bridge are available.

Black and yellow bands may be added to bridge arches or girders and parapet walls to improve the conspicuity of the bridge.

Roundels or warning triangles will sometimes be incorporated into advance direction signs which may also indicate an alternative route to take to avoid the low bridge.

*

*

Roundels may also be incorporated into road works signs to indicate temporary height restrictions.

Where the reduced headroom over a road is due to an overhanging building a plate may be added below the warning triangle to indicate this.

*

Level Crossing Signs and Signals

Before the crossing

Level crossing without a gate or barrier

*

STOP when lights show

Advance warning of light signals at a level crossing with a gate or barrier

Drivers of LARGE or SLOW VEHICLES must phone and get permission to cross

LARGE means over 55′ long or 9′6″ wide or 38 tonnes total weight SLOW means 5 mph or less

At automatic level crossings the drivers of large or slow vehicles must phone before and after crossing

*

DRIVERS OF LONG LOW VEHICLES phone before crossing

Long low vehicles may be at risk of grounding and drivers of such vehicles must phone before crossing

NEW LEVEL CROSSING CONTROL AHEAD

New method of controlling traffic at a crossing ahead

Where a level crossing is concealed, countdown markers indicate the distance to the stop line

Safe height 16′-6″

Electrified overhead cable and the safe height beneath it

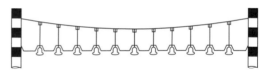

Bells suspended over the road to give an audible warning to drivers of vehicles which exceed the safe height beneath electrified overhead cables

At the Crossing

ANOTHER TRAIN COMING
if lights
continue to show

* Some crossings have flashing red road traffic signals - these mean STOP (and this applies to pedestrians too). A steady amber light shows before the red lights begin to flash, as at ordinary road traffic signals; this means STOP unless it is unsafe to do so. If the red lights flash for more than three minutes without a train arriving or any half-barrier is lowered without the lights flashing, phone the signalman. If your vehicle breaks down or stalls on a crossing without barriers or with barriers only halfway across the road, get yourself and your passengers out of the vehicle, phone the signalman and then, if he says there is time, push the vehicle clear. Stand well back if audible warnings and lights start.

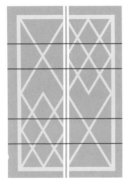

Yellow box markings indicate an area of carriageway at a level crossing which must be kept clear. Do not enter the box if other stationary traffic may cause you to stop with any part of your vehicle within the box.

* Flashing pedestrian signals used at some level crossings to indicate that it is not safe to cross and pedestrians should stop at the pedestrian stop line.

Direction to phone

Location of phone

TO CONTACT BR
phone
0181-123-4567

Phone number by which you can contact the rail operator

PARK HERE AND USE PHONE AT CROSSING

Place where drivers of large or slow vehicles should park near an automatic level crossing while seeking permission from the signalman to cross

Automatic half-barrier level crossings

Amber lights and audible warnings followed by flashing red lights warn that a train is approaching and that the barriers are about to come down. You must STOP. The red lights flash all the time the barriers are down. If another train is approaching the barriers will stay down and the lights will continue to flash and the sound of the audible warning device change in character.

Level Crossings with Miniature Red/Green warning lights

These level crossings have gates or barriers but no attendant. The miniature red and green lights are operated by an approaching train. Full directions for using these crossings are given on roadside signs.

Open Level Crossings

The St. Andrew's cross is used at all level crossings without either gates or barrier.

*

Automatic open level crossings have flashing road traffic signals and audible warnings. The lights will flash and the warnings sound until the train(s) have cleared the crossing.

If there is more than one railway line over the crossing, this signal will also flash and the sound of the audible warning will change in character if another train is approaching.

You must always STOP when the traffic light signals show.

Open level crossings without gates, barriers or road traffic light signals have give way signs over a symbol of a railway engine.

You must always look out for, and give way to trains.

Tram Signs and Signals

Trams can run on roads used by other vehicles and pedestrians. The part of the road used by trams (the 'swept path') may have a different colour or textured surface to the rest of the road, or it may be edged with special road markings. *The 'swept path' must be kept clear.* Trams cannot move out of the way of other road users.

Route for trams only

Warning of trams crossing the road ahead

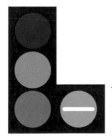

Reminder to pedestrians to look out for trams approaching from both directions

Warning signals for pedestrians. The lights flash when a tram is approaching

Drivers of other vehicles must give way to trams at level crossings without barriers or gates. Sometimes just a "Give way" sign and a tram plate may be used

Examples of signals and signs for tram drivers

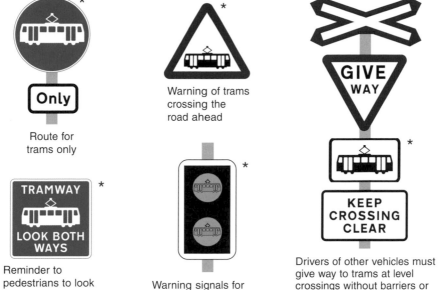

Stop

Proceed ahead

Proceed left

Proceed right

Stop unless it is unsafe to do so

Speed limit sign for tram drivers (All diamond shaped signs are only for tram drivers)

The signal mounted to the right gives instructions to tram drivers which may not be the same as those given to drivers of other vehicles

Bus and Cycle Signs and Signals

Route for buses and pedal cycles only

BUS LANE
LOOK RIGHT *

Reminder to pedestrians to look out for buses or buses and pedal cycles approaching from the right

BUS AND CYCLE LANE
LOOK RIGHT *

Up to 31.12.96:
No vehicles with over 12 seats (excluding driver) except scheduled bus services, and school and works buses.
From 1.1.97:
No vehicles with over 8 seats (excluding driver) or local buses

Bus lane road marking

With-flow bus lane ahead which pedal cycles and taxis may also use

Contra-flow bus lane

Arrow used to show direction of possible traffic movements at the end of a bus lane

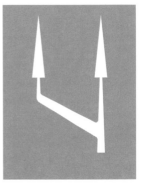

With-flow bus and pedal cycle lane sign showing hours of operation

End of bus lane

Bus and cycle lane *

Contra-flow bus and pedal cycle lane on road at junction ahead

Bus lane

Bus lane on road at junction ahead

Bus Stop

Stopping place
for buses

*

Stopping place
for tourist buses to
allow passengers
to take
photographs

Bus stop
where other
vehicles are
prohibited
from stopping

Bus stop

*

Stopping place for buses operated by
London Transport

Parking place for buses

*

Place where buses
may stand, from
which other vehicles
are prohibited during
times shown

Stopping by vehicles
other than buses
prohibited during
times shown

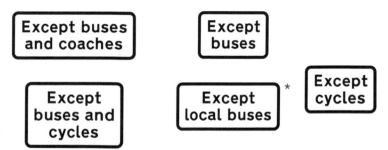

Plates used to indicate exemptions for bus and pedal cycles
from prohibitions such as turn left ahead and no left turn

31

Route for pedal
cycles only

Shared route for
pedal cycles and
pedestrians only

Separated track
and path for pedal
cycles and
pedestrians

Route recommended
for pedal cycles

With-flow pedal
cycle lane

Riding of pedal
cycles prohibited

Pedal cycle
route ahead

Contra-flow pedal
cycle lane

With-flow pedal
cycle lane ahead

CYCLISTS
DISMOUNT

Pedal cyclists to
dismount at end of, or
break in, pedal cycle
lane or route

Light signals for control
of pedal cycles

Child cycle
tests

Training or testing child
pedal cyclists on road
ahead

END OF
ROUTE

End of pedal cycle
lane or route

Cycle lane

Pedal cycle lane on road
at junction ahead or pedal
cycle track crossing road

Except
cycles

No through route except
for pedal cyclists

CYCLE LANE

LOOK RIGHT

Reminder to pedestrians to
look out for pedal cycles
approaching from right

Cross
section *

Road marking between
separated pedal
cycle/pedestrian route

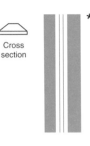

Parking place for
pedal cycles

Pedal cycle lane
road markings

END

End of pedal cycle
lane road markings

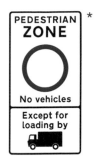

Pedestrian Zone Signs

Areas such as shopping streets may be signed as Pedestrian Zones. Depending on the extent of the vehicle entry restrictions, such areas may be paved without the usual separation between footway and carriageway and may not have yellow lines and kerb markings to indicate waiting and loading restrictions. Instead restrictions are detailed on zone entry signs and repeater plates. Various examples of the zone entry signs are shown below.

Where different restrictions apply at different times of the day and these restrictions are too complicated to show on a time plate, a sign which can change its display (a variable message sign) may be used. It is therefore important always to check the restrictions in force before entering the zone.

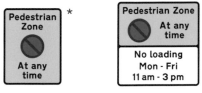

Two examples of repeater signs

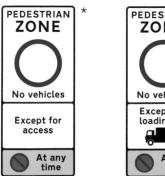 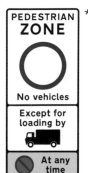

At the end of the zone a "zone ends" sign will be displayed

Waiting and Loading Restrictions Signs and Road Markings

Waiting Restrictions

Waiting restrictions are indicated by both signs and road markings. The restrictions usually apply to the whole of the highway including verges and footways.

Yellow lines along the edge of the carriageway, parallel to the kerb, indicate that restrictions are in force. In environmentally sensitive areas a paler shade of yellow may be used and the width of the lines may be reduced. Changes are being introduced to simplify the present system. By January 1999, the broken yellow line will be replaced by a single solid yellow line or a white bay marking depending on whether waiting is prohibited for a short period or allowed for a limited period only.

Small yellow plates are normally erected adjacent to the carriageway to give more precise details of the times of operation of the restrictions. If a Bank Holiday falls on a day when restrictions are in operation, the restrictions will apply in the normal way unless the plate specifically states that they will not. It is therefore important always to check the plates as well as the markings.

Waiting prohibited 24 hours a day, 7 days a week, for at least 4 consecutive months

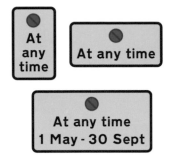

Waiting prohibited for any shorter period. The arrow indicates the direction in which the prohibition starts

This No Waiting sign is used on portable signs to mark temporary waiting restrictions

Controlled Zones

In controlled zones the entry signs give details of the times and days the restrictions operate. The sign may also indicate that the zone is a Meter Zone, Disc Zone, Ticket Zone, Voucher Parking Zone or Pay and Display Zone. Inside the zone, yellow lines show where waiting is prohibited or restricted. No yellow time plates are provided unless the waiting restriction imposed on that particular length of road is different from that indicated on the zone entry sign.

Entrance to Meter
Zone

Entrance to Voucher
Parking Zone

End of Controlled or
Voucher Parking Zone

Parking bays inside the zone are marked on the carriageway with white lines and any conditions of parking appear on meters, ticket machines or upright signs.

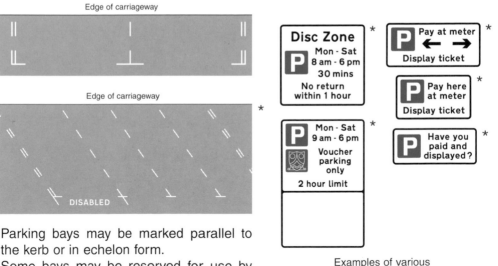

Parking bays may be marked parallel to the kerb or in echelon form.

Some bays may be reserved for use by disabled people and this will normally be shown on the carriageway.

Examples of various
upright signs

Where a parking area is only available for a limited time or limited use, for example, by local residents, disabled badge holders, doctors or large or slow vehicles, road markings and upright signs will show this. Various examples are illustrated below.

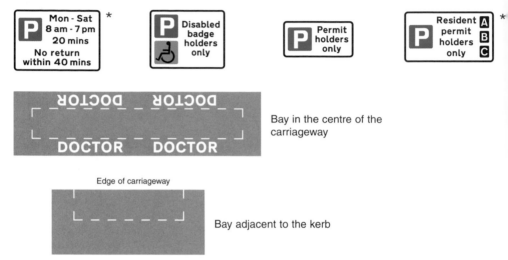

Bay in the centre of the carriageway

Edge of carriageway

Bay adjacent to the kerb

In some areas local authorities operate special goods vehicle waiting restrictions. Usually these apply to goods vehicles of over 5 or 7.5 tonnes maximum gross weight. Where the same restrictions apply throughout a zone, details of the restrictions are given at the beginning of the zone and may be repeated within it, but there are no special road markings.

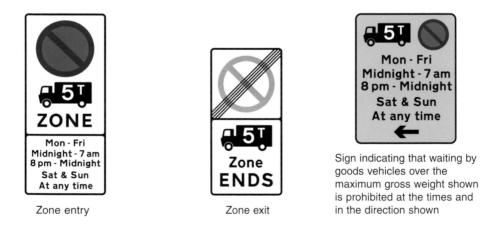

Zone entry

Zone exit

Sign indicating that waiting by goods vehicles over the maximum gross weight shown is prohibited at the times and in the direction shown

There are equivalent signs for buses with the bus symbol, and signs which apply to both goods vehicles and buses.

Loading Restrictions

Where waiting is restricted or prohibited but there is no prohibition on loading, a time limit is often in force. This is usually 20 minutes and is not shown on the signs. Yellow kerb marks, together with black and white plates, indicate loading restrictions ("loading" means unloading as well!). When loading is not taking place the waiting restrictions must be observed. As with yellow lines, changes are being introduced to simplify the present system. The new meanings for the kerb marks and plates are given below, but some of the existing marks and signs will remain until 1 January 1999. Remember always to look at the plates as well as the markings to see what restrictions apply.

Loading restrictions in force 24 hours a day, 7 days a week for at least 4 consecutive months

No loading at any time

Loading restrictions in force for any shorter period. The arrow indicates the direction in which the prohibition starts

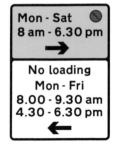

Loading Areas

Off-highway areas may be designated "loading areas" where waiting is restricted except by permitted vehicles. Signs are used without road markings to indicate this.

Sign at entrance to loading area

Repeater sign within area

End of loading area

Loading Bays

Edge of carriageway

LOADING ONLY

Loading only

*

Where waiting and loading are generally prohibited, special loading bays may be indicated by a broken white line "bay" marking with the words "LOADING ONLY" and a sign with a white on blue "trolley" symbol.

Clearways

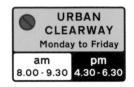

URBAN CLEARWAY
Monday to Friday

am	pm
8.00 - 9.30	4.30 - 6.30

URBAN CLEARWAY
End

End of urban clearway

The "No Stopping" sign means no stopping on the main carriageway (except at a layby) at any time – not even to set down passengers

In built up areas, urban clearways may be provided. During the times the urban clearway is in operation, no stopping is allowed on the carriageway or verges, except for as long as may be necessary for setting down or picking up passengers (but waiting restrictions may apply at other times)

No stopping except in emergency

Yellow lines will not be used with clearway signs in future

Stopping in a layby not allowed, except in an emergency. These laybys usually have an emergency telephone

There are other places where stopping on the carriageway is prohibited.

At **schools**, you must not stop on the road markings – even to set down or pick up children or other passengers.

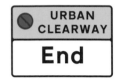

No stopping
Mon - Fri
8 am - 5 pm
on school entrance markings

*

SCHOOL — KEEP — CLEAR

At **taxi ranks**, other vehicles may be prohibited from waiting or stopping.

| No waiting 11 pm - 5 am except taxis * | No stopping 11 pm - 5 am except taxis * |

Edge of carriageway

Stand for 3 taxis *

Information boards may be provided at taxi ranks.

Stationary vehicles are to be kept clear from the **entrances to off-street premises**, or where the kerb is dropped to provide a convenient **crossing place for pedestrians.**

At certain **bus stops** other vehicles may be prohibited at certain times, but as a general rule you should not park at any bus stop.

Edge of carriageway

No stopping 7 am - 7 pm except buses

Bus stop with stopping prohibition

Edge of carriageway

Bus stop without stopping prohibition

Road Markings

At junctions with traffic signals

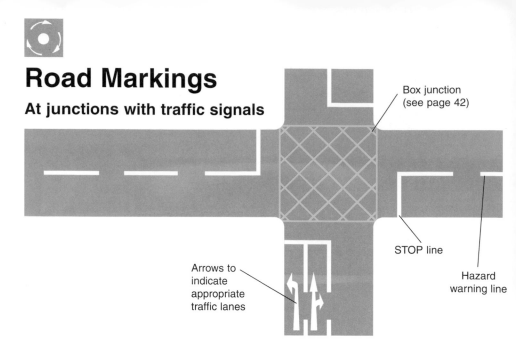

Box junction (see page 42)

Arrows to indicate appropriate traffic lanes

STOP line

Hazard warning line

At junctions where traffic must STOP or GIVE WAY

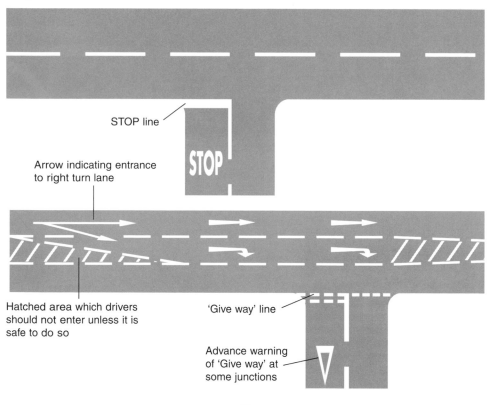

STOP line

Arrow indicating entrance to right turn lane

STOP

Hatched area which drivers should not enter unless it is safe to do so

'Give way' line

Advance warning of 'Give way' at some junctions

At Roundabouts

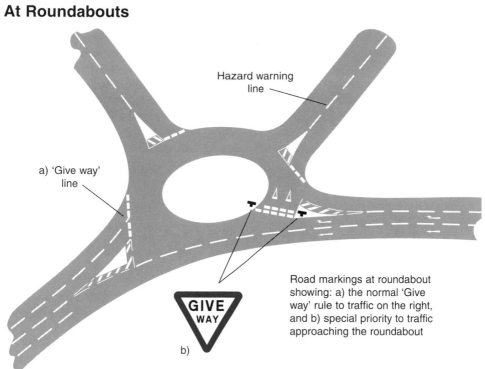

Hazard warning line

a) 'Give way' line

GIVE WAY

b)

Road markings at roundabout showing: a) the normal 'Give way' rule to traffic on the right, and b) special priority to traffic approaching the roundabout

At Mini-Roundabouts

Although mini-roundabouts do not look quite like normal roundabouts, you must give way at the broken white line to traffic from the right and drive round the roundabout in a clockwise direction. Large vehicles may drive over part of the central circular marking if necessary to negotiate the junction.

The mini-roundabout is placed before the 'Give way' line – it means drivers must give way to traffic from the right and circulate clockwise

At some locations the 'Give way' sign will be shown above the mini-roundabout sign. In these cases the triangular road markings and double 'Give way' lines will be used

Across the Road

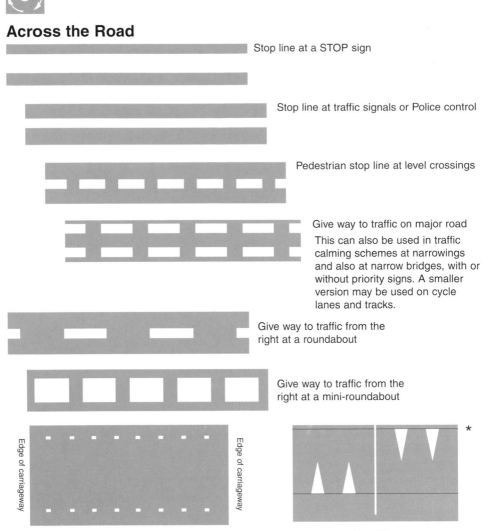

Stop line at a STOP sign

Stop line at traffic signals or Police control

Pedestrian stop line at level crossings

Give way to traffic on major road

This can also be used in traffic calming schemes at narrowings and also at narrow bridges, with or without priority signs. A smaller version may be used on cycle lanes and tracks.

Give way to traffic from the right at a roundabout

Give way to traffic from the right at a mini-roundabout

Edge of carriageway

Edge of carriageway

*

Road hump

The most suitable place for pedestrians to cross a road where traffic is controlled by signals or where traffic is subject to control by the Police or a traffic warden

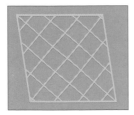

Where it is likely that stationary traffic could block the road, a yellow box may be marked on the road, covering all or part of the junction. You must not enter the box if your exit is not clear, except if you want to turn right and are only prevented from doing so by on-coming traffic or other stationary vehicles waiting to turn right.

Along the Road
Double White Lines

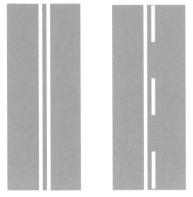

These are used to separate opposing traffic flows where visibility is restricted. Viewed in the direction of travel, if the line closest to you is continuous you must not cross or straddle the line (except to turn into or out of a side road or property or to avoid a stationary vehicle blocking your lane or to overtake a pedal cycle, horse or road works vehicle moving at not more than 10 mph). Where the line closest to you is broken, you may cross the lines to overtake if it is safe to do so.

Diagonal Lines

Diagonal white lines (hatched markings) may be used to separate traffic lanes, to protect traffic turning right, or along the nearside or offside edge of carriageway. Where an area is bordered by a continuous line you must not enter the hatched area. Where the line is broken, you should not enter the area unless it is safe to do so.

Diverge Arrows

This type of arrow is used to indicate a place where traffic streams divide.

Deflection Arrows

These arrows are used to indicate the direction in which traffic should pass double white lines and hatched markings or the route high vehicles should take under a low arch bridge.

Lane Markings

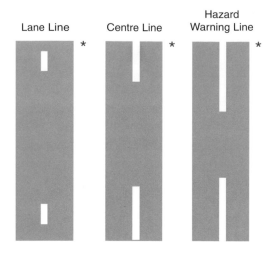

Lane Line *   Centre Line *   Hazard Warning Line *

Various lane markings are used. As a general rule, remember the more emphatic the marking the greater the hazard.

Chevron Marking

Part of carriageway where traffic passes in the same direction on either side of the chevron marking and should not enter unless safe to do so

On a motorway, part of the verge or hardshoulder between the main carriageway and a slip road where traffic passes on either side in the same direction and where traffic must not enter except in an emergency

44

Along the Edge of the Road

Edge of carriageway other than at junctions, exits from private drives and laybys

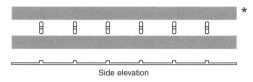

Side elevation

Alternative edge of carriageway marking with raised ribs for motorways and all-purpose roads with hard shoulders or strips, which provides an audible and tactile warning

Edge of carriageway at junctions, exits from private drives and laybys, or the division between the main carriageway and a traffic lane which leaves the main carriageway at a junction ahead, or, where laid diagonally, the start of a traffic lane

Edge of main carriageway at junctions and exits from private drives or, where laid diagonally, the start of a pedal cycle lane

Reflecting Road Studs

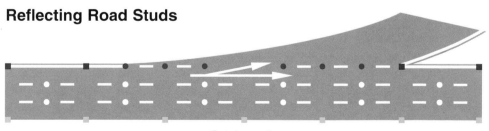

Central reservation

These help drivers at night or in poor visibility. White studs mark traffic lanes or the centre of the road, while the edge of the carriageway is marked by red studs on the left hand side and amber studs by the central reservation on dual carriageways. Green studs are used to mark the entrances to and exits from slip roads and laybys.

Other Markings

Used with upright sign and white line

Associated with various hazards

May be used with upright sign

Do not block that part of the carriageway indicated

Indication of a compulsory movement

Indication of traffic lanes for particular destinations

Warning of "Give way" just ahead

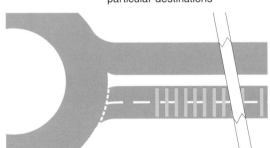

Transverse yellow bar markings used to slow traffic on the approach to roundabouts

Marks on the road to indicate the limits of a measured length of road to enable the police to assess the speed of traffic

Direction in which pedestrians should look for approaching traffic

Edge of carriageway

Motorway Signs and Signals

Most motorway signs have a blue background with white lettering, numbers and borders, but tourist attraction signs on motorways have brown backgrounds (see page 53).

Special traffic regulations govern the use of motorways. These include: no stopping (except in an emergency, on the hard shoulder or verge), no U-turns, and no reversing. Goods vehicles with a maximum gross weight of more than 7.5 tonnes, buses longer than 12 metres, and vehicles drawing trailers must not use the right hand lane of a motorway which has three or more lanes. Motorways must not be used by certain classes of traffic – learner drivers other than HGV, invalid carriages of less than 254 kg unladen weight, pedal cycles, motorcycles under 50 cc capacity, agricultural vehicles, and vehicles incapable of attaining a speed of 25 mph on the level when unladen and not drawing a trailer. Pedestrians and animals are also prohibited.

This sign indicates where motorway regulations
start to apply to the road

Direction signs to a motorway indicating the route
number and destination. Where the motorway
symbol is included, motorway regulations apply from
that junction. The junction number may also be
shown on these signs

In order to ensure that direction signs are absolutely clear to drivers travelling at motorway speeds it is necessary to limit strictly the number of destinations shown. Therefore, when planning a motorway journey it is always advisable to check the junction number of the exit you require before setting off. Junctions can be identified by the number shown on a black background in either the bottom left hand or top left hand corner of motorway signs.

Motorway junction numbers are usually shown on road maps, so it is easy to check these before starting out on your journey. Then, when on the motorway, junction numbers can be used as a guide to your location.

There are three main signs for each junction:

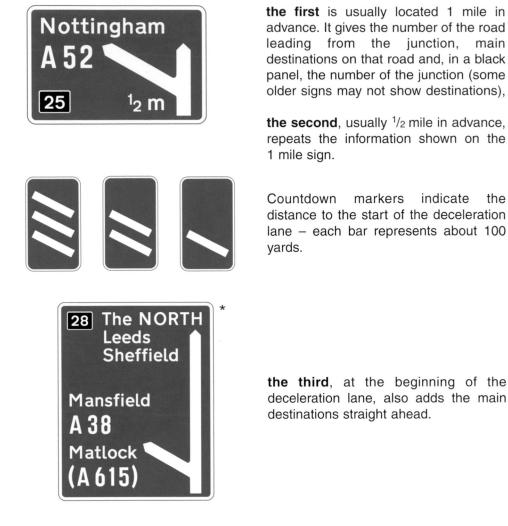

the first is usually located 1 mile in advance. It gives the number of the road leading from the junction, main destinations on that road and, in a black panel, the number of the junction (some older signs may not show destinations),

the second, usually ¹/₂ mile in advance, repeats the information shown on the 1 mile sign.

Countdown markers indicate the distance to the start of the deceleration lane – each bar represents about 100 yards.

the third, at the beginning of the deceleration lane, also adds the main destinations straight ahead.

A final route direction sign is usually located at the separation of the exit slip road from the main carriageway.

Where two junctions follow in quick succession, signs 1 mile and ½ mile in advance of the first junction may indicate the destination and route to which each junction leads.

At the start of each deceleration lane the normal "third" sign will show the number of the road leading from the junction, the main destinations reached by leaving the motorway at that point, the main destinations straight ahead, and, in a black panel, the particular junction number.

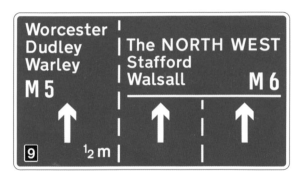

Where the left hand lane of a motorway leads only to another motorway or route at the junction ahead (and there is a reduction in the number of lanes on the main carriageway) the 1 mile and ½ mile signs will show the destination and route to which each lane leads, as will...

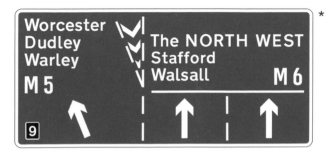

*

the sign where the two routes diverge. Countdown markers are not used at this type of junction.

*

Where the junction ahead is with another motorway, an additional sign, usually 2 miles in advance, may be provided.

At junctions where additional lanes join the motorway, signs may indicate the number of lanes, the direction from which they are joining and which traffic lanes take priority. These signs may also show the distance to the point where the lane(s) join.

On main carriageway

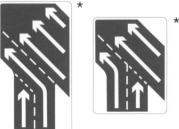

On slip road or joining lanes

Once past a junction, a route confirmatory sign will give the main destinations ahead, with the distances to those destinations shown in miles.

On some motorways, signs are placed on gantries over the road. The principle – three main signs for each junction – is the same. The junction number and distance to the junction are shown on the gantry below the sign.

Where there is no loss of lane beyond the junction the upper part of the sign containing the inclined arrow indicates the destinations reached via the slip road, while the lower part of the sign containing the upright arrow shows the destinations on the main carriageway. Any lane may be used to continue straight ahead.

Where there will be a reduced number of lanes available on the main carriageway beyond the junction – for example, three lanes before the junction but only two after – downward pointing arrows directly under the sign mean "select your destination and get in lane". Countdown markers are not used at this type of junction.

 *

Where there is a possibility that a junction sign could become overloaded with destinations, additional, separate signs may be used to advise motorists of the route to be followed for destinations which cannot otherwise be accommodated on the main junction sign.

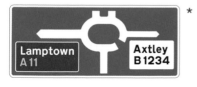 *

On the slip road leading from the motorway, a blue and white map type sign will show the destinations reached along the joining routes. Where the joining route is a primary route, the destination will be shown on a green panel; where the joining route is a non-primary route, the destination will be shown on a white panel.

 *

Where a motorway terminates at a roundabout ahead, again the destinations reached along the subsequent and joining routes will be shown on coloured panels appropriate to the class of each route.

Sometimes, a slip road from a motorway leads only to a maintenance compound, signed as a works unit, and is not open for general use.

Observation platforms are sometimes provided at the back of the hard shoulder. These may only be used by the Police.

 *

Where a motorway has been widened but the original bridges retained, there may be no hard shoulder through the bridge. Where this occurs, signs will indicate the distance over which this applies.

On most motorways, service areas are provided at intervals of not more than 30 miles, half an hour at normal motorway driving speeds. These service areas are open 24 hours a day, every day of the year and they must provide fuel and free parking and toilets. Refreshments, telephones, disabled access and other facilities, such as motels and Tourist Information Centres, may also be provided.

At about 1 mile in advance of a motorway service area, a sign will indicate the availability of services ahead with the distances and the names of the operators.

At about ½ a mile in advance of a motorway service area a large sign will show the operator's name (at the top), the name of the service area, and, by the use of various symbols, the facilities provided there. The price of petrol is shown per litre. A green pump symbol on a white panel indicates that the price shown relates to unleaded petrol. This may be replaced by the four star symbol where appropriate.

The start of the deceleration lane is indicated by a third sign. These signs may show the operator's name.

A final sign is located at the separation of the deceleration lane from the main carriageway. A similar sign may also be used to indicate which exit to take when a service area is accessed from a roundabout off the motorway.

Services
10 m

After each motorway junction, another sign may indicate the distance to the next motorway service area. Where a junction with another motorway will be reached before the next motorway service area, the distance to the next motorway service area(s) on that motorway will also be shown.

Tourist attraction signs on motorways have brown backgrounds.

*

On the main carriageway of the motorway, brown background signs may indicate tourist attractions, geographical areas or towns containing Tourist Information Points or Centres, which can be reached by leaving the motorway at the next junction. These signs are normally at $3/4$ and $1/4$ mile from the junction.

*

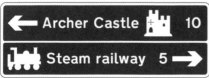

On the slip road leading from the motorway, a brown background sign will indicate the route to take to reach the tourist attraction shown.

For more information on tourist information signs and the symbols used, see pages 65 to 67.

Black background signs on motorways indicate routes advised for goods vehicles which differ from the routes to be used by other vehicles.

The location of County, or in Scotland, Regional boundaries may be signed.

On motorways, emergency telephones which are connected directly to the police, are located at the back of the hard shoulder at about one mile intervals. The telephone boxes are orange and white (orange and black in some places). If you need to use an emergency telephone because your vehicle has broken down or because of some other emergency, you will be asked for the number shown on the box. This number enables the police to pinpoint your location so that assistance can be provided quickly.

Marker posts are located at the back of the hard shoulder at about 100 yard intervals and show the direction to the nearest emergency telephone.

At the entrance to a motorway service area, maintenance compound or other similar facility, this sign is used to indicate the point at which motorway regulations cease to apply.

This sign indicates that the motorway ends in 1 mile

This sign marks the end of the motorway

On motorways, signals are located on the central reservation, at the back of the hard shoulder or on gantries over the road.

Signals located on the central reservation or at the back of the hard shoulder apply to drivers in all lanes. Signals over the road apply only to drivers in the lane below that particular signal.

Normally, signals are blank, but in abnormal conditions they are switched on either by the Police, in an emergency, or automatically by, for example, fog. These signals tell drivers what action they should take or what conditions they should expect ahead.

Four amber lights flash in alternate horizontal pairs to provide a warning and to draw drivers' attention to the message displayed. Flashing red signals mean drivers MUST STOP if prevented from joining another lane. Where shown at the entrance to a motorway, drivers must not enter the motorway.

Sometimes, the reason for a restriction shown on a signal may not be apparent when first seen. There may have been an accident ahead, so take no chances – obey the signals.

Signals on the central reservation or at the back of the hard shoulder

Various lane closures

Temporary maximum advisory speed limit   Leave at next junction   Risk of fog ahead   End of restriction

Signals on gantries over the motorway

Temporary maximum advisory speed limit

Change lane

Leave motorway at next exit

* Risk of fog ahead

* Stop, all lanes ahead closed

* Stop, all lanes ahead closed

* Stop, all lanes ahead closed

* Do not proceed any further in this lane

* End of restriction

Signals at the entrance to a motorway

All lanes ahead closed, do not enter the motorway

Signals on older motorways

On older motorways you may encounter this type of signal.

It indicates that there is a hazard ahead. Do not exceed 30 mph until you have passed the hazard.

Primary Route Direction Signs

Routes of primary traffic importance form a national network between major towns. These are called **Primary Routes**. Along these routes, the next primary traffic destination and the route number are shown on the signs. Maps often pick out the primary destinations, thus enabling drivers to note, when planning their journey, the destinations which will appear on the signs.

On all primary routes the direction signs have a green background, yellow route numbers and white lettering and border.

On a long journey away from the motorway, follow the green signs.

For many years, blue panels have been used on signs on the approaches to motorways. The Traffic Signs Regulations and General Directions 1994 further extended this system of colour coding. Panels and patches coloured according to the class of road along which a destination is reached may now be incorporated into all advance direction signs except those on the main carriageway of a motorway. (A motorway slip road sign incorporating coloured panels is shown on page 51.)

For simple junctions and where space is restricted, destinations can be "stacked" on advance direction signs. The blue panel and motorway symbol indicate that motorway regulations will apply at the junction in the direction shown.

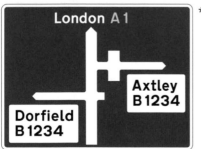

For more complex junctions, a "map" type sign will show the junction layout. The thickness of the lines on the sign indicate the importance of the roads leading from the junction. The white panels show that these exits from the junction are non-primary routes.

On main roads, major junctions have an advance direction sign some way before the junction. Where there are too many destinations to show on one sign, there will be two advance direction signs. The first will usually show major destinations and the second will show more local destinations. Both signs will have a green background.

*

Junction names may be shown at the top of advance direction signs to help drivers to identify where they are. These signs may also incorporate a brown background tourist information sign as a panel. The blue patch shows the direction to a motorway.

On dual carriageway primary routes with grade separated (multi-level) junctions, signs are usually provided at least ¹/₂ mile in advance and repeated at the beginning of the deceleration lane. Some junctions have an additional sign 1 mile in advance.

*

Countdown markers may also be used to indicate the distance to the start of the deceleration lane – each bar represents about 100 yards.

Another sign is usually sited at the junction, marking the turn. These signs are in the appropriate colour for the route they are pointing towards.

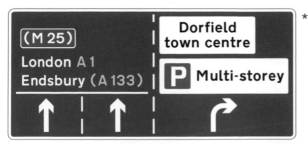

Lane information may be given on advance direction signs. Directions to car parks are also shown on white panels.

Signs may also give advance indications of prohibitions or warn of hazards.

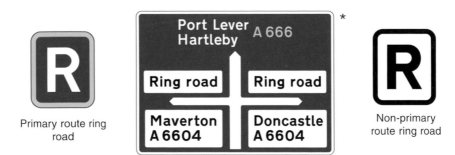

Primary route ring road

Non-primary route ring road

Ring roads (which can be primary or non-primary routes) bypass town centres. Ring roads may be indicated on advance direction signs and "R" repeater signs may also be placed along the route.

Signs may indicate towns or villages that have been bypassed.

On busy roads, signs may be placed on gantries over the road

Where there is no loss of lane beyond the junction the upper part of the sign containing the inclined arrow indicates the side road destinations while the lower part of

the sign containing the upright arrow shows the destinations on the main carriageway. Any lane may be used to continue straight ahead.

* Where there will be a reduced number of lanes available on the main carriageway beyond the junction – for example, three lanes before the junction but only two after – downward pointing arrows directly under the sign mean "select your destination and get in lane". Countdown markers are not used at this type of junction.

On main carriageway

On slip road

Where additional lanes join the road, signs may indicate the number of lanes, the direction from which they are joining and which traffic lanes take priority.

Once past a junction, a route confirmatory sign may give the main destinations ahead, with the distances to those destinations shown in miles. In some cases it may be necessary to turn onto a different route ahead to reach the destination. (Older signs show these destinations in brackets.)

Non-Primary Route Direction Signs

Existing blue-bordered local direction signs will be phased out, since research showed that there was not a clear understanding of the distinction between these and the black-bordered non-primary route signs. In future, signs on all routes other than motorways or primary routes will have white backgrounds and black lettering, numbers and borders.

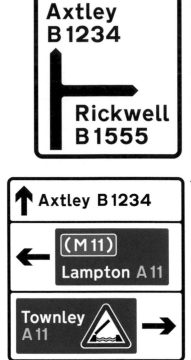

Non-primary route signs may include panels and patches coloured according to the class of road along which a destination is reached.

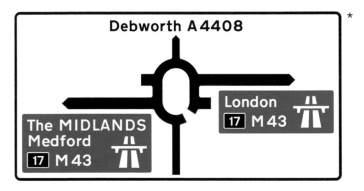

As for primary route signs, the thickness of the lines on non-primary "map" type signs indicates the importance of the road leading from the junction. The blue panel and motorway symbol indicates that motorway regulations will apply at the junction in the direction shown. The motorway junction number may be shown on the blue panel. A green panel indicates a primary route leading from that junction.

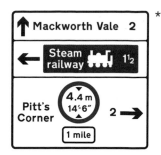

Junction names may be shown at the top of non-primary route direction signs to help drivers to identify where they are. These signs may incorporate a brown panel indicating the direction to a tourist attraction and may give advance warning of hazards ahead and indications of restrictions. The distance in miles to a destination may be shown,

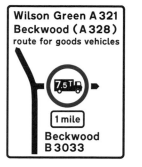

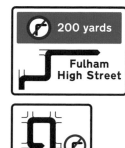

and they may give advice on alternative routes.

Non-primary route signs may incorporate directions to hospitals (see page 78), toilets, ferries, railway and bus stations, parking areas and other facilities. Red bordered panels show the direction to Ministry of Defence establishments (see page 77). The small roundabout symbol indicates a mini-roundabout.

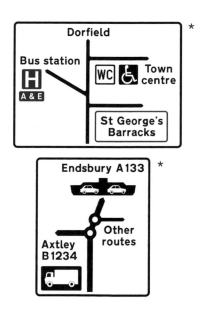

A shopping area providing a service for the disabled, approved by the National Federation of Shopmobility

Railway station (the Passenger Transport Executive symbol may be varied)

Dual carriageway non-primary routes with grade separated (multi-level) junctions usually have advance signs at least ½ mile before the junction. Where the left hand lane leads only to another route (a lane drop junction), these advance direction signs will show the route and destination to which each lane leads.

 *

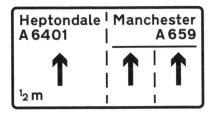

On busy roads, signs may be placed on gantries over the road.

 *

Countdown markers may be used to indicate the distance to the start of the deceleration lane. They are not used at lane drop junctions. At junctions where additional lanes join the road, signs may indicate the number of lanes, the direction from which they are joining and which traffic lanes take priority. These are similar in design to the motorway signs shown on pages 48 and 50 and to the primary route signs shown on pages 59 and 61, but they are black and white.

A sign with a chevron and pointed end is sited at the junction, marking the turn.

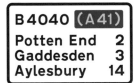

A non-primary route may also have route confirmatory signs...

...and be a ring road.

 *

Where there is a possibility that a junction sign could become overloaded with destinations, additional signs may be used to advise motorists of the route to be followed for destinations which cannot otherwise be accommodated on the main junction sign.

64

Tourist Signs

Distinctive white and brown signs are used to help direct travellers to tourist attractions and facilities. Examples of the tourist attraction signs used on motorways are shown on page 53.

Symbols, some of which are illustrated below, are used to denote different types of attraction.

Tourist Information Point

Castle

Historic House

National Trust Property

Zoo

Wildlife Park

Country Park

Air Museum

Pleasure or Theme Park

Agricultural Museum

Motor Museum

Site of Roman Remains

Shire Horse Centre

Vineyard

Engish Heritage

Flower Garden

Nature Reserve

Prehistoric Site or Monument

Industrial Heritage Museum

As an alternative to a symbol indicating the type of attraction, a general tourist attraction symbol may be used:

 *

in England the symbol used is a rose,

 *

in Scotland the symbol used is a thistle, and

 *

in Wales the symbol used is a dragon.

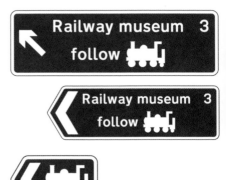

Travellers may be advised to follow signs showing a particular symbol to an attraction.

At junctions, repeater signs showing the symbol alone may be used.

 *

Where there is no suitable symbol, a worded sign may be used.

Advance direction signs on primary, non-primary and local routes may also incorporate a brown background tourist sign as a panel. Examples of these can be found on pages 59 and 63.

Tourist signs may indicate the directions to several attractions...

the location of a Tourist Information Point or Centre...

*

and may also give directions to a route of special interest or a route which passes through an area of special interest.

*

Some tourist signs give the distance ahead to the attraction.

*

*

Information boards may also be used to provide details about tourist attractions and facilities in nearby places or areas.

*

Services Signs

Information about direction signs to motorway service areas is given on page 52.

Service areas on primary and non-primary routes may be signed where toilets, fuel, refreshments, telephones and parking are available at least between 8 am and 8 pm on every day except Christmas Day, Boxing Day and New Year's Day. Green background signs are used on primary routes and white background signs on non-primary routes.

Primary route services sign

Where these service areas are open 24 hours a day the phrase "not 24 hrs" is omitted.

Where services are provided only for goods vehicles the phrase "Lorries only" is shown. Where services are not provided for goods vehicles a crossed out lorry symbol is shown.

The spoon and fork symbol denotes a restaurant; the cup symbol denotes that light refreshments are available.

A double pump symbol indicates that both leaded (four star) (black pump) and unleaded (green pump) petrol are available.

The symbols indicating facilities for the disabled and the availability of tourist information may be added where appropriate.

The bed symbol may also be added to these signs where an hotel or motel is provided.

Non-primary route services sign

In addition to the advance direction signs shown above, further signs will be sited at the entrance to the service area, marking the turn.

Where services in a small town or village are provided off the main route, signs at the junction will indicate the direction in which they are located and may indicate the distance. (In some cases a brown sign may be used.)

Direction to a public telephone

Direction to a Royal Automobile Club telephone

Direction to an Automobile Association telephone

Direction to public toilets which have facilities for disabled people

Picnic areas, licensed camping and caravan sites and youth hostels managed by the Youth Hostels Association or the Scottish Youth Hostels Association may be signed with distinctive brown background signs.

Picnic area

Youth Hostel

Camping and caravan site

Picnic area with parking, toilets, Tourist Information Point or Centre, public telephones and a viewing point

Direction Signs for Pedestrians and Cyclists

Where a route recommended for pedal cyclists and/or pedestrians is different from the route for other vehicles, special white on blue direction signs showing the cycle and/or pedestrian symbol may be provided. Special direction signs for cyclists may be incorporated as a blue panel into primary and non-primary route direction signs as shown below. Signs for pedestrians may also be other colours especially in town centres or on country footpaths.

Separate special direction signs for cyclists may also be provided before junctions...

at a junction with a route recommended for cyclists or pedestrians...

and these signs may indicate that the recommended route is shared by cyclists and pedestrians.

71

Pedestrian route to a tourist attraction

Pedestrian route to a car park associated with a tourist attraction

These signs are used to show the way to a cycle parking place

These signs show the direction to, or route along, a public footpath or bridleway (Alternative designs and colours may be used)

A waymark, used to indicate the direction to take along a footpath, bridleway or byway (Alternative colours may be used)

Parking Signs

Parking places are signed with the familiar white "P" symbol on a blue background. This symbol may be incorporated into primary and non-primary direction signs, as shown below and on page 60, or shown on separate parking place direction signs.

Distance to parking place ahead

Signs may indicate that the parking places ahead are only for a particular type of vehicle, such as goods vehicles...

cars...   and caravans...

or the particular type of parking place in the direction indicated...

P

or that use of the parking places is restricted in some way.

The total number of parking places available may be shown in the bottom right hand corner of the panel...

and variable message signs may be used to indicate whether parking places are available.

Signs can also show where "park and ride" schemes operate.

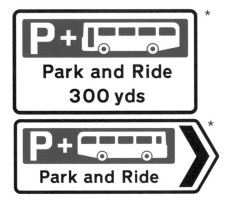

Other Direction Signs

Temporary diversion routes

Where it is necessary to close a section of motorway or other main road to traffic in an emergency, special signs may be displayed to advise drivers on that road, or wishing to join it, of the alternative route to follow to rejoin the original road past the point of closure. If the alternative route is relatively easy to identify and follow, the route number may be shown on the special signs. No additional signs will be placed along the route.

However, where the alternative route is complex, drivers may be advised to follow a special symbol (which is either incorporated in existing direction signs or displayed on separate signs along the route) until the original road is rejoined or until permanent signs indicating the route to that road are picked up.

Examples of the diversion route symbols

Where it is necessary to divert traffic temporarily onto another route, black and yellow signs may be used to mark the alternative route to be followed.

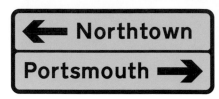

Emergency Signs

Routes for emergency vehicles to temporary incident control points are marked with red and white signs.

The signs used to mark the route for emergency vehicles to permanent incident control points have light green backgrounds, white lettering and yellow borders.

The same colour combination is used for signs which indicate the direction to emergency pedestrian exits in tunnels...

and to mark the location of fire rendezvous points.

Emergency telephones

 *

Where emergency telephones are provided on roads other than motorways, signs such as this will indicate their location. Information on motorway emergency telephones is given on page 54. A sign with the 'P' symbol indicates that parking is only provided for use of the emergency telephone.

Non-motorway direction signs

Signs to Ministry of Defence establishments have distinctive red borders and direction arrows.

 *

Where a route recommended for lorry drivers is different from the route for other vehicles, white on black signs will indicate the advisory route. These signs may incorporate route numbers on coloured patches.

 *

Direction to a Department of Transport testing station for goods vehicles.

A modern version of the traditional finger post has been introduced for use on minor rural roads. Some signs may have square ends and they may include a distance in miles.

NEWTON LONGVILLE *

 *

Special black and yellow temporary signs may now be used to indicate the location of new housing developments. These signs may be left in place for up to six months after completion of the development.

Information Signs

Signs for pedestrians

Ramped entrance to pedestrian footbridge or subway

Stepped entrance to pedestrian footbridge or subway

One-way traffic in the direction indicated

Police signs

These temporary signs are put out by the police to warn of potential danger or accident ahead, and the need to proceed with caution.

In an emergency, these signs may be used to advise traffic to use the hard shoulder as a running lane and when traffic must rejoin the main carriageway.

Hospital signs

Hospitals without accident and emergency facilities will be shown by a blue and white "H" symbol.

Hospitals with accident and emergency facilities will be shown by a red and white "H" symbol.

Vehicle checks

These temporary signs are put out when vehicles are to be stopped for an excise licence check or vehicle condition inspection.

Goods vehicle checks

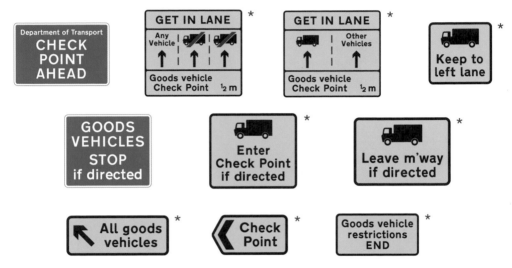

These signs are used to warn that spot checks are taking place, that goods vehicles may be directed to enter the check point and that they should keep in the lane indicated.

Traffic Surveys

These signs are used to warn that traffic surveys are taking place and that vehicles may be directed to stop at the census point.

Signs giving information about the road layout ahead

Distance to the start of dual carriageway road ahead

Section of dual carriageway road begins directly ahead

 *

Distance over which a short length of dual carriageway road (which begins directly ahead) extends

No through route for vehicular traffic ahead

No through route for vehicular traffic in direction indicated from junction ahead

Road ahead only wide enough for one line of vehicles, but passing places are provided at intervals

 *

Passing place on a narrow road

Road unsuitable for type of vehicle shown which may include lorries, buses and caravans

Number of traffic lanes reduced ahead (the background colour will be green on primary routes and blue on motorways for permanent signs)

Junction ahead where left hand lane is for traffic turning left and must not be used by other traffic except buses

Boundary signs

HERTFORDSHIRE

County

**ARUN DISTRICT COUNCIL
ARUNDEL**

Town or village

Haven District Council
Welcome to
AXTLEY
Please drive carefully
Twinned with Cedant   *

Town or village

These signs may include a crest or logo, a message of welcome, a phrase about a local geographical or historical feature, or a road safety message.

Miscellaneous

**Priority over
oncoming
vehicles**   *

Traffic travelling in the direction indicated by the large white arrow has priority over traffic travelling in the opposite direction

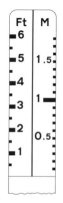

Depth of water at a ford shown in metric and imperial units

**Try
your
brakes**

**Keep in
low gear**

**Escape lane
ahead**   *

Escape lane ahead for vehicles unable to stop on a steep hill

Department of Transport approved vehicle test centre

**MOTORCYCLE
TEST CENTRE**   *

Motorcycle test centre

Entrance to and exit from a private access road or property

Entry to and exit from a private access road or property to or from a public road not allowed

81

Traffic Signals

In most cases, in addition to the primary signals at the stop line, there are duplicate signals, known as secondary signals, located on the opposite side of the junction. If the primary signal is not working, you must obey the secondary signal as if it were the primary.

RED means STOP. Wait behind the stop line on the carriageway until GREEN shows

RED & AMBER also means STOP. Do not pass the stop line until GREEN shows

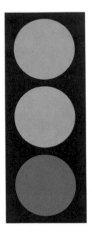

GREEN means go IF THE WAY IS CLEAR

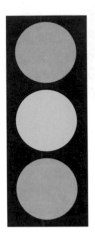

AMBER means STOP. You may only go on if the amber appears after you have crossed the stop line or are so close to it that to pull up might cause an accident

Signs may also be placed with traffic signals to qualify the meaning of the green signal by prohibiting a turning movement or instructing traffic to move only in a certain direction.

Additional white light signals may be provided for tram drivers (see page 29).

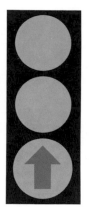

If movement is allowed only in one direction, a green arrow pointing in that direction may replace the full green signal. Again, signs may be used with these signals to reinforce the message of the green arrows.

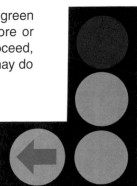

Green arrows may also be provided in addition to the full green signal if movement in a certain direction is allowed before or after the full green phase. If the way is clear, you may proceed, but only in the direction shown by the green arrow. You may do this whatever other signals may be showing.

When the green arrow and full green signal are shown, you may turn right while opposing traffic is held at a red signal. At the same time, the full green signal allows the movement of traffic in other directions.

Alternative design of green arrow

*

Tidal Flow Lane Control Signs and Signals

On some busy roads, lane control signals are used to vary the number of lanes available to give priority to the main traffic flow.

Special signs give advance warning of lane control signals...

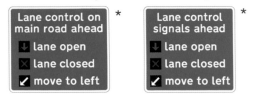

and explain the meanings of the signals shown.

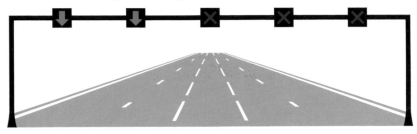

The lane control signals are displayed over the road to indicate the availability of the various lanes. A red cross means that the lane is closed to traffic facing the signal. A white diagonally pointing arrow means that the lane is closed ahead and traffic should move to the next lane on the left. A green downward pointing arrow indicates that the lane is available to traffic facing the signal.

Alternative design of red cross

Alternative design of green arrow

Alternative designs of white diagonal arrow

A sign will also indicate the end of a controlled section.

Pedestrian Crossings

Zebra crossings

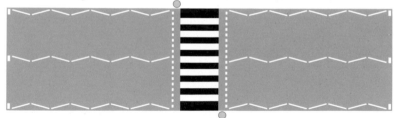

Drivers: It is an offence to park or wait within the area bounded by the extremes of the zig-zag markings – you may stop only to give way to pedestrians on the crossing or in circumstances beyond your control.

Within the zig-zag area, you must not overtake the moving motor vehicle nearest the crossing or the leading vehicle which has stopped to give way to a pedestrian on the crossing.

When giving way to pedestrians, you should stop at the broken 'give way' line about a metre (yard) short of the crossing.

Pedestrians: You should always cross on the striped crossing – never on the zig-zag area.

Pelican crossings (pedestrian controlled)

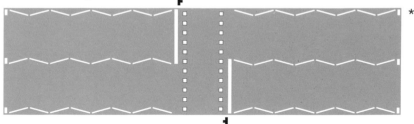

Drivers: It is an offence to park or wait within the area bounded by the extremes of the zig-zag markings.

If the AMBER or RED signals show, you should stop at the stop line about a metre (yard) short of the crossing.

As at ordinary traffic signals, GREEN, AMBER and RED signals are shown to drivers but RED and AMBER do not appear together at a Pelican crossing. Instead, FLASHING AMBER is shown. This means give way to pedestrians; only proceed if the crossing is clear.

Pedestrians: You should always cross on the crossing between the studs – never on the zig-zag area.

Pelican crossings have special red, green and flashing green signals for pedestrians which are operated by a push button. The signals are on the other side of the road facing you as you cross.

Wait   Cross with care   Do not start to cross

Signal controlled junctions

Red and green signals for pedestrians which are operated by a push button are provided at many signal controlled junctions. Again, the signals are on the other side of the road facing you as you cross.

Wait   Cross with care

Puffin crossings

Gradually, a new type of pedestrian crossing, called a Puffin, will be used in place of most Pelicans and the pedestrian phase at new signal controlled junctions. Puffins do not have a flashing amber and flashing green pedestrian phase. Pedestrians use a push button box similar to the one shown but with the red and green pedestrian signals mounted above it, on the same side of the road. Puffins have the added advantages that the pedestrian crossing time is automatically varied according to the actual needs of the pedestrian and, if after the push button has been pressed the pedestrian decides not to cross and walks away, the

call is automatically cancelled and the pedestrian phase will not appear. Therefore, Puffins not only offer better protection for pedestrians but also remove the irritation drivers now feel if needlessly stopped at signal controlled pedestrian crossings when no pedestrians are waiting to cross.

Toucan crossings

A new shared use crossing, called a Toucan, has been developed which can be used by both pedestrians and cyclists together. Cyclists may ride across Toucans whereas they must dismount at other crossings.

Road Works Signs

The road works ahead sign gives drivers advance warning of road works or a temporary obstruction of the carriageway ahead. The works may be large scale motorway maintenance schemes or the lamps being changed in a set of traffic signals.

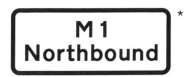 *

A plate may be shown with the road works ahead sign to explain the nature or the location of the works.

Traffic cones may be used to mark the edge of the route for vehicular or pedestrian traffic through or past a temporary obstruction.

Barriers are used to mark the boundaries of an area of the highway closed to vehicular and pedestrian traffic.

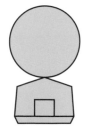

At night or in poor daytime visibility road danger lamps may also be used to indicate to traffic the limits of a temporary obstruction of the carriageway.

Major works on motorways and other main roads

From time to time essential maintenance and road improvements must be carried out, but whilst these works are taking place it is also necessary to keep traffic flowing as freely as possible. In order to do this various traffic management techniques can be used. Traffic can be marshalled into narrow lanes or a reduced number of lanes. Some or all lanes may be diverted to the other carriageway; this technique is known as contra-flow.

Advance warning signs

"Courtesy" signs are provided to give advance notice of the location, start date and expected duration of future major road works or advance warning of the nature of the works and of possible delays at current major road works.

 *

Signs may be provided before the works begin to warn drivers that delays may occur in the near future, thus giving them an opportunity to allow more time for future journeys, to look for an alternative route or to make some other arrangements for the duration of the works.

Signs may sometimes be placed well in advance of the works to give drivers an opportunity to use an alternative route.

When the works begin, signs giving information about the scheme may be provided.

 *

Signs indicating the nature of the work and the possibility of delays will be placed 2 miles and 1 mile, respectively, in advance of the actual road works.

* In the interests of road safety, temporary mandatory speed limits are now imposed at all major road works sites. A sign will normally be placed about ¾ mile in advance of the point where this speed limit comes into effect.

Signs showing which lanes are available through the works are placed 800, 600, 400 and 200 yards in advance of the works. Examples are shown below.

The two right hand lanes of a four lane dual carriageway are closed 800 yards ahead. The two left hand lanes remain open.

200 yards ahead the right hand lane is closed. The left hand and centre lanes remain open and the hard shoulder may be used as a running lane.

800 yards ahead the middle lane of a three lane single carriageway road is closed.

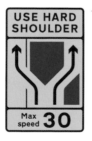

Traffic using the left hand lane should move to the hard shoulder, traffic using the centre lane should move to the right hand side of the carriageway. An advisory speed limit of 30 mph is in operation.

Traffic using the left hand lane should move to the hard shoulder, traffic using the right hand lane should move to the other carriageway.

Alternatively, when there is a need to segregate traffic through the works, signs showing the restrictions applicable to or destinations reached via each lane are placed 800, 600, 400 and 200 yards in advance of the works. A number of examples follow:

800 yards ahead traffic wishing to leave the motorway should be in the left hand lane, vehicles over 7.5 tonnes must not use the right hand lane.

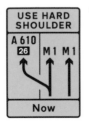

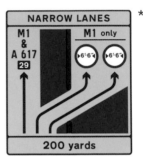

800 yards ahead traffic is diverted from the left hand and centre lanes to the hard shoulder and left hand lane.

400 yards ahead lanes are narrower than usual. Vehicles wider than 7' 6" must not use the right hand lane.

200 yards ahead the centre and right hand lanes are diverted to narrow lanes on the other carriageway. Vehicles wider than 6' 6" must not use these narrow lanes. Traffic wishing to leave the motorway should use the left hand lane.

Traffic wishing to leave the motorway should use the hard shoulder.

Advance warning of a junction where the permanent sign is obscured by road works (sign used on roads other than motorways).

Advance warning of a junction where the permanent sign is obscured by road works (sign used on a motorway).

Cones and "keep left" or "keep right" arrows will be used to marshal traffic into appropriate lanes and signs will advise drivers to stay in the lane they have chosen.

Signing through the road works

At the crossover point at the beginning of a section of contra-flow, chevrons may be used to indicate a sharp deviation of route.

Chevron

Traffic cylinders, reflecting road studs, barriers, delineators and cones may be used to keep traffic in appropriate lanes, to indicate the edge of a route for traffic and to protect the work force.

Traffic cylinder

Sharp bend ahead where traffic is diverted on to a temporary road for a short distance

Additional signs will be placed at intervals to remind drivers which lanes are open to traffic and in which direction traffic should be travelling in each lane. These signs may also show the distance over which these conditions apply.

Where it is necessary to change the traffic management arrangements part way through the road works, signs will again advise drivers of the need to move to a different traffic lane or carriageway.

Where it is necessary for works vehicles to gain entry to or exit from the works site itself, there may be a break in the line of cones, cylinders or barriers to enable them to cross to or from the running traffic lane. These entry/exit points are marked with special red and white signs as shown below.

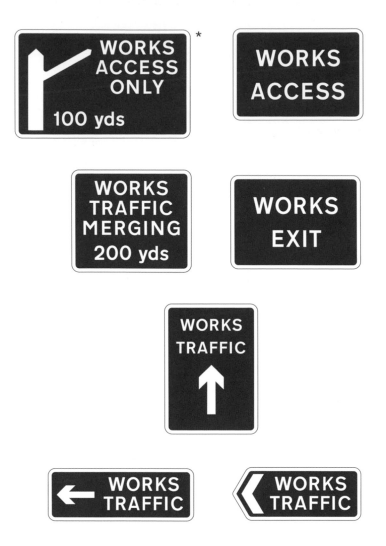

These signs not only tell the drivers of works vehicles where these entry/exit points are located but also serve to alert other drivers to the need to proceed with extra care, to allow for vehicles which may be moving slowly prior to gaining access to the site, or after emerging from the site.

Where junctions occur on a length of road on which road works are in progress, signs may indicate that a lane will leave the main carriageway at the junction, or that an additional lane will join the main carriageway after the junction, or that joining traffic will merge with traffic already on the main carriageway. These signs may also indicate the distance to the lane drop, lane gain or traffic merge.

 * * *   *  *

Signs on main carriageway

Signs on joining slip road

At the end of the road works, signs direct drivers back onto the original carriageway. These signs may also show the distance to the point where this manoeuvre should commence.

 *  *  *

End of narrow lanes

 *  *

End of hard shoulder running

Once traffic has returned to the main carriageway a sign will mark the end of the road works and any temporary restrictions (such as speed limits). This may also carry a message of apology for any delays caused.

Mobile [...] ways and other dual carriageway roads

Sometim[...] be carried out on motorways and other dual
carriagew[...] [...]ed for road closures or major traffic
manageme[...] [...]d by carrying out the work from a slow-
moving or s[...] [...]s, signs are mounted on the back of the
vehicle or ve[...] [...]orks and/or lane closures ahead. The
plates used w[...] [...]ing sign may explain the nature of the
works (for exan[...] [...]ing") or the effect of the works (for
example "lane cl[...] *[...]ones or other delineators used on
the road.*

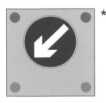

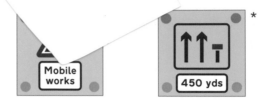

*

When a slow moving or stationary vehicle blocks a traffic
lane, a keep left or keep right arrow will be mounted on the
back of the vehicle to indicate the direction in which other
traffic should pass the obstruction.

When signs are mounted on the back of vehicles in this way, they are
accompanied by four amber lamps which flash in alternate horizontal pairs.

*These signs will not be displayed while the vehicle is travelling at normal speed
on its way to or from the road works site.*

Other vehicles involved in maintenance work should
display a sign with the legend "Highway Maintenance"
or "Motorway Maintenance" as appropriate. A single
flashing amber lamp may be displayed (usually on

**HIGHWAY
MAINTENANCE**

the roof of the vehicle, which may be a private car). The light from this lamp will
be visible from all directions at a reasonable distance from the vehicle.

Mobile road works on other roads

Vehicles involved in mobile works on other roads, for example grass cutting, weed
spraying, road sweeping, sign maintenance or gritting, may display a "road works
ahead" warning sign with a plate explaining the nature of the works taking place.
A single flashing amber lamp may be displayed (usually on the roof of the
vehicle). The light from this lamp will be visible from all directions at a reasonable
distance from the vehicle.

Road works on single carriageway roads

*

"Courtesy" signs may be provided to give details about the nature of the work, the names of the employer and contractor and a telephone number to call in an emergency.

On single carriageway roads, road works may completely block one side of the road. If it is not possible to divert the traffic that would normally use that side of the road to an alternative route it is then necessary to operate shuttle working.

This can, over very short lengths, be achieved by having manually operated stop/go boards at each end.

Over longer lengths, portable traffic signals are used to control the traffic flow. Where portable traffic signals are used, you must not proceed past this sign unless the green signal is showing and the way ahead is clear, or if the amber signal appears when you are so close to the sign that to pull up might cause an accident.

If a side road joins a road on which portable signals are operating but it is not itself controlled by such signals, this sign will warn drivers on the controlled road...

and this sign will warn drivers on the side road.

Pedestrian signs

On single carriageway roads and urban dual carriageway roads it may also be necessary to make special provisions for pedestrians. A temporary route or crossing point may be provided together with a sign indicating the route pedestrians should take.

Miscellaneous warning and informatory signs for road works

Traffic signals not in use

Zebra, Pelican or Puffin
crossing temporarily out of use

 *

Variable message sign ahead
not in use or being tested

Temporary absence of road
markings for distance indicated

 *

Temporary absence of hard
shoulder for distance indicated

Temporary sudden change
in level of carriageway

Temporary hazard, vehicular
traffic should proceed slowly

Loose chippings on the road.
This sign is usually shown with
an advisory speed limit

Temporary warning of
permanent change in road
layout ahead

Traffic Calming

Traffic Calming is the term used to describe physical features provided at regular intervals along a road to encourage people to drive their vehicles at a lower speed than they might otherwise have done. As well as conventional devices, such as roundabouts, traffic calming schemes can employ a variety of measures, including road humps and narrowings. Appropriate warning signs will normally indicate the type of measure to be expected.

Road humps in direction and for the distance shown

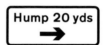

Road hump in direction and at the distance shown

Road humps may have a flat or round top, extending across the width of the road or covering a whole junction. They may also be in the form of a "cushion", only covering part of a traffic lane and designed for vehicles to straddle. Other than in a 20 mph zone, warning signs are erected at the beginning of the road where the hump or series of humps are installed.

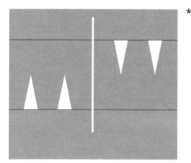
*

Each road hump will normally be marked with triangle and edge line markings, though in 20 mph zones this is not required.

Zebra and Pelican Crossings can be installed to coincide with a flat top hump. In advance of these locations additional warning signs may be installed.

97

Roads may be narrowed by the use of "build outs" on one or both sides. When placed on both sides they may be opposite each other or staggered. Warning signs indicating the side the narrowing occurs may be used in advance.

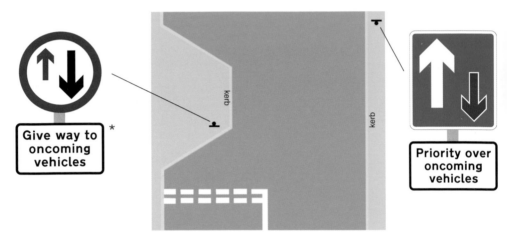

At the narrowings give way markings may be laid on one approach to give priority through the narrowing to traffic coming from the opposite direction. These markings may be accompanied by priority signs. It is essential that drivers do obey the signs and markings and allow priority to drivers coming from the opposite direction.

If priority is not given to any particular direction then drivers should ensure that they can pass through the narrowing without endangering occupants in vehicles approaching from the other direction. Drivers should not accelerate on the approach to a narrowing, but maintain a slow steady speed, be prepared to give way to approaching traffic and let any cyclists proceed ahead of them.

Some traffic calmed areas are indicated by a 20 mph speed limit sign. A 20 mph sign, as well as indicating the speed limit, also warns that within the zone drivers will meet road humps, or narrowings, or other features, and it is likely that these will not be individually signed. It is important that in these areas drivers adopt a steady but low speed, and avoid frequent acceleration or deceleration.

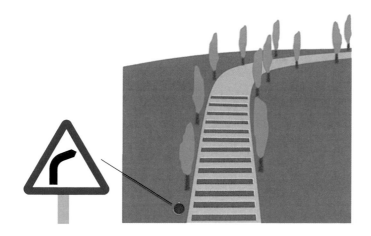

Rumble devices, either in the form of strips or areas across the road, are often used in rural areas to provide a vibratory and audible effect. The intention is to alert drivers to the hazard ahead and encourage them to reduce their speed before encountering the hazard. A warning sign may be used in association with the rumble device to identify the hazard. Rumble devices are not normally specifically signed.

Textured or coloured road surface

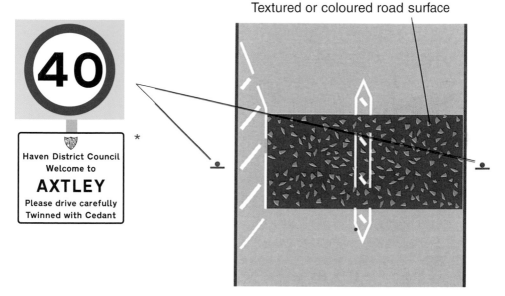

Gateways into villages may be formed from a combination of speed limit signs, yellow backing boards and village name plates. Central hatched markings or islands may also be used to separate opposing flows. Drivers approaching the gateways should reduce their speed and observe the speed limit all the way through the village.